HOME TURF
ANN MATTHEWS

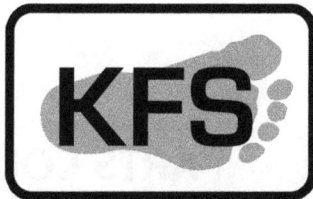

KFS

Newton-le-Willows

Published in the United Kingdom in 2020
by The Knives Forks And Spoons Press,
51 Pipit Avenue,
Newton-le-Willows,
Merseyside,
WA12 9RG.

ISBN 978-1-912211-56-2

Acknowledgements are due to the editors of the following magazines in which some of these poems first appeared: *Tears in the Fence*, *Shearsman Magazine*.

Home Turf is inspired by Lyn Hejinian's My life and started as a much shorter and unrefined 'Finding Myself in the World of Places'.

A large thank you to the large cast of past and present friends and family who have shared places and experiences with me.

LOTTERY FUNDED

Supported using public funding by
ARTS COUNCIL ENGLAND

Dedicated to
Maeyc and Sue Hewitt

CONTENTS

Each poem in *Home Turf* represents a place I have lived or attended in chronological order. They comprise a specific number of lines that relate to the name or street number of each abode and the time spent at that location. My memories are bound with and dislocated from these places. Memory is not factual, it is made up of snippets, miscellaneous moments that are wholly subjective. The universal truth of them should always be questioned. But it is a fact that most of us have addresses, homes where we eat, live, lay down our heads and dream of the places and experiences that we have known, are yet to know, or may never know . . .

Can form make the primary chaos (the raw material, the unorganized impulse and information, the uncertainty, the incompleteness, vastness) articulate without depriving it of its capacious vitality, its generative power? Can form go even further than that and actually generate that potency, opening uncertainty to curiosity, incompleteness to speculation, and turning vastness into plenitude? In my opinion, the answer is yes: that is in fact, the function of form in art. Form is not a fixture it is an activity.

— **Lyn Hejinian (The Rejection of Closure)**

zero plus

9

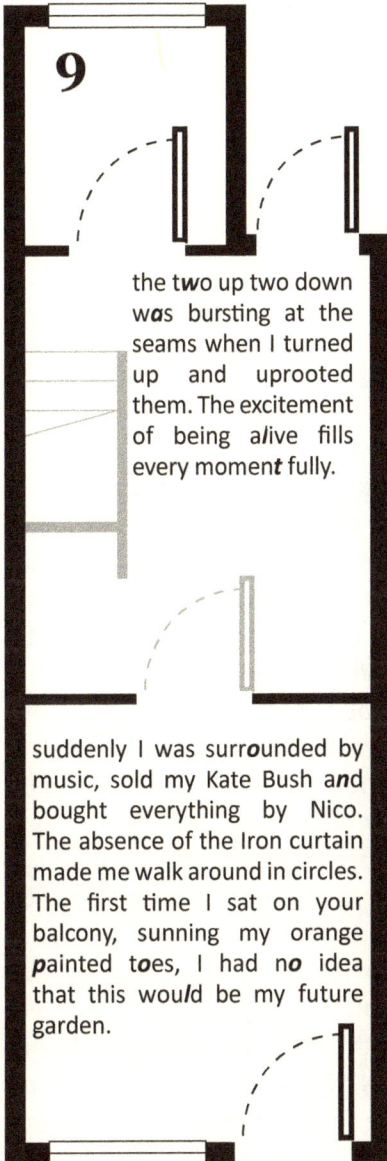

the two up two down was bursting at the seams when I turned up and uprooted them. The excitement of being alive fills every moment fully.

suddenly I was surrounded by music, sold my Kate Bush and bought everything by Nico. The absence of the Iron curtain made me walk around in circles. The first time I sat on your balcony, sunning my orange painted toes, I had no idea that this would be my future garden.

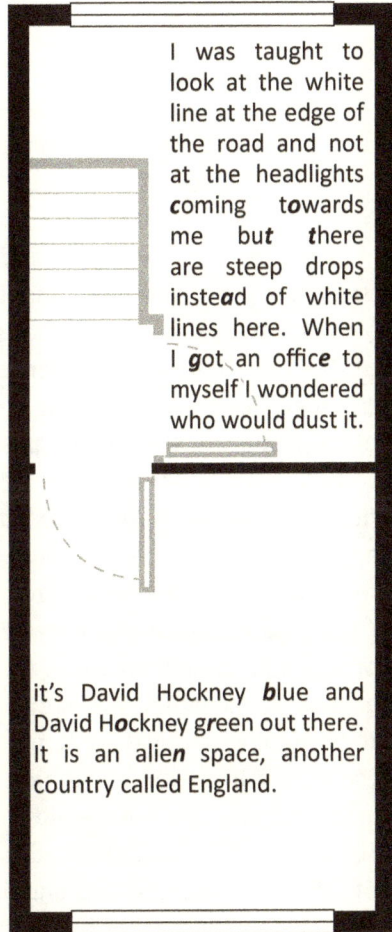

I was taught to look at the white line at the edge of the road and not at the headlights coming towards me but there are steep drops instead of white lines here. When I got an office to myself I wondered who would dust it.

it's David Hockney blue and David Hockney green out there. It is an alien space, another country called England.

7

being
the devil's
advocate can lead
you   places   that   are
sometimes refreshing. My favourite
place is a home, not a building. I was
in my Bronte phase that summer when I snuck
out in my white nighty and walked bare foot through the
drenched grass and the candyfloss dawn mist. By now Dover is
almost a second home. I'm not sure whether the sheep and ghosts
of Tre Ceiri enjoyed our version of free-jazz on saxophone and
trumpet. Serial monogamy is a dirty occupation and not a label to
be tagged with. I burnt my past, eight bin bags of writing, which
turned into a feathery pile of ash, though some words escaped and
fluttered over south Anglesey. Dad measured out peanuts in identical
eggcups and we thought it best not to argue. What is time but your
measure. This is the second recession that I have lived through but
I can't distinguish a gap between them. Picking magic mushrooms
on the school field was fun, though I'd run away and curl up with
a good book when you consumed them. We seemed to follow
the Fasching carnival from north to south Germany, beating out
the winter in unison. Even nice people can be bad losers. Thunder
crashes once, light bulbs shatter and the green light screams like my
sister. In the hot and tinder-dry bowl of the Hungarian plain herds
of thin sheep bleated and undulating shoals of grey mice scattered.
My subjectivity is part of who I am. I was fascinated by the intense
lime-green and shiny finger-sized dips of the buttons on my cardigan.

six - seventeen

10

the
sparrow
hawk flashed
through the *b*ack d*o*or a
millisec*o*nd after the blackbird
and *t*humped her thwack *o*nto th*e*
carpet and off they s*w*ept before *y*ou coul*d*

bat an eyeli*d*. Whatever method*s* are prescribed, you can't make me eat mus*h*y peas. The sn*o*w clings t*o* b*l*ack br*a*nches. 'Becoming an arc*h*itect when I was y*o*ung was prohibi*t*ively expensive and the preserve of the elite so I *b*ecame a t*e*acher instea*d*,' she said with a l*o*ng sigh. I*f* there is an afte*r*life you'll be in gr*e*at company. It was hard work fighting *o*ver ch*o*res but being a *l*atch-key kid came with its freedoms. Beer bottles are good for slide gu*i*tar, *t*hough *i*t's less messy if y*o*u dri*n*k the beer first. We got to wondering wh*a*teve*r* happened to Radio Rentals and the idea that *y*ou didn't need to buy everything. 'Paws!' then the to*w*elling *o*f ea*r*s. Spee*d*ily they went through their *s*upply *of* spare clot*h*es before h*a*ving a spec*t*acular water fight – ***probably their first*** – then spent the rest of the day in their pyjamas.

9 trad

tears
seldom fall.
It's never the *same*
two days runnin*g*. Happy
neighb*o*urs who say sorry a lot do*n*'t
have mas*t*iffs that lean over the wall
bar*k*ing at visitors. Studying *t*akes you in
spirals. I had a recu*r*ring night*m*are
where a friend with evil inten*ti*ons crept
in thro*u*gh my bedroom wi*n*dow years
before I saw his twi*n* Bob *i*n Twi*n* Peaks.
Tabitha Limbird – a new porn star? You
can walk here but you can't actually *g*et
any*w*here. Aunty knows she's si*tt*ing on
a stoo*l* in her kitchen but *d*oes not
know who she is ta*l*king to. I watch th*e*
*d*rinkers eg*g* *e*ach other on *wit*hout
meaning to.

11

hidden behind blank registers are the efforts to know everything that forgets what IS and what's NEXT. This year the sycamore is the last to lose its leaves. 'Roll your shoulders in both directions.' The channel M-shapes across the estuary cutting off walkers who head inland instead of sideways. Don't sit next to me – I need to stretch all the way to Liverpool. This shortlist includes sweet pea seeds and digitalis. There's fly eggs on the edges of dead ears. I saw your name scratched in sand. Heresy is fine. Land is just a string of description. Silence is slippery – a cold currency.

8

those are the wheels and
that's the world. A sloping
longman stands staff in hand.
Once again, the loveliness of a
pink puppy belly wins me over.
It was a sore summer drinking
through straws and aiming for
a normal temperature. The
furore of water

throws up mists and rainbows
as we stand on the banks of
the Rhein at Schaffhausen.
There's words to speak in this
frozen moment. She served us
Tunisian tomato stew with
poached eggs amongst mad
cats and spotless French
friends. A lesson plan slips
into the future.

No. fifty one

(Wk 1)

not all of these memories are mine,
they are stolen, you say, from
photographs. What are crushes but
tools to get you through those
empty moments. My parents were
flabbergasted when they found
broken glass under the carpet and
someone's bike up the pear tree
and subsequently banned her from
hosting parties. In the middle of the
back of Czechoslovakia wolves
howled to the full moon, an August
storm ran in, a river burst its banks,
I cowered in a leaking tent whilst
the others whooped in the rain.
Learning their names, their sizes
and their correct places in the tool
shed meant that I could pass the
right spanners to my father as he
lay under the Volkswagen. When
you meet your match you can run
away or face him square on and
embrace her . . .

(Wk 2)

. . . I brace myself against the lashing wind, peer eyes half shut through the hailstones and whistle. Never expect him, however much he says he loves you, to take you home to meet the family. She gave me her pocket money wrapped in a multi-coloured drawing of a deer-donkey. The Telecaster left my hand, arced speedily through the air, missed him, hit the concrete and broke into two splintery pieces. The boats with bright billowing spinnakers are mirrored perfectly in breathless water. I'm stuck in time-bubbles where dreaming takes on another dimension. Unaware that it wasn't the done thing, I snuggled between them on their first honeymoon morning . . .

(Wk 3)

. . . before getting into bed each
night a ladder was raised and with
vacuum hose in hand we sucked up
the spiders that snuck along *the*
black beams. We shrank crisp
packets with lighters and much
patience in the pub on the corner.
Trying to lift her by her thin loose-
skinned arms without bruising her
still hurts something. I pushed him
in a buggy until he slept and saw a
male echo of myself. Perched on
the parapet of an old stone bridge I
convinced you it wasn't at all
dangerous. He caught every yellow
budgie that our neighbour bred, not
one green nor blue, and left them
mangled on our doorstep . . .

(Wk 4)

. . . you catch crabs by lifting
seaweed covered boulders,
grabbing them swiftly with finger
and thumb just above their middle
legs where they can't pincer you. It
is comforting to know that there
are others who fear getting locked
in toilets. A child will catch it if they
are found with shallow glasses of
bubbling champagne however
mesmerised they are by the army
of tiny airy globes that rise to the
surface. We don't like sport but we
invariably beat our German friends
at table-football. Mum told me to
stop being so imaginative but the
tone of her voice didn't convince
me. The thinnest cotton-thread
seaweed is the slipperiest and the
greenest . . .

(Wk 5)

. . . Patti Smith beat her frail chest
whilst she sang, Nico cried *until* her
mascara ran and dripped off her
chin, Courtney Love threw out
bottles of water *to* her gasping
fans, Kim Gordon looked like an ice
queen, Bjork squatted on stage
without apology and PJ Harvey
crooned like Sinatra on speed. The
boot is on a difficult foot and it
hurts a *great* deal. There was an
East Germany, a place that you
entered with a visa and where old
women dressed from head to foot
in black cackled with mirth when
you fell over on the ice and landed
your arse. I design in curves. It was
the Baron Hill energy vampires *that*
did it – though I *don't* believe in
them – the dog bolted *and* a week
later her name tag arrived in the
post, found in a place we had never
been to. I stood balanced on one
foot and missed the bus – the
pavement was teeming with
ladybirds . . .

(Wk 6)

. . . in the plastic-fumed heat of a cheap hire car we explored the black and rusty lumps and bumps of an empty landscape and wound our way to the volcano where tourists rode crotchety camels with bad breath. Dyed white sheets black and his clothes came out mottled grey for weeks afterwards. The tarn had the greenest grasses peeking through its surface and millions of turquoise dragonflies hovered enchantingly. The sore fingers and fume induced headache were worth the creative satisfaction of melting toy soldiers on a two-bar electric fire and remoulding them into peaceful citizens. My introduction to the possibilities of communal living made me promise to live alone and never to consume brown rice and lentils at the same sitting. I miss standing on tippity-toes to reach gran's sweet-violet powder-puff and her glorious Sunday hat . . .

(Wk 7)

. . . in Prague we came across a
young soldier crying – the country
we had entered was a different one
to the one we would exit. I sported
a swimsuit in the bright nylon
fashions of the 70s, my uncle, a
casualty of the late 60s, drew
matching pink and blue daisies in
the gaps on my belly. The best bit
was drawing contour maps,
including all the relevant symbols,
with a set of finely sharpened
colour pencils. The sparrow hawk in
Broughton screeches spectacularly
like a creature being tortured. Life
ends like this: the drink-driver hits
him and drags him twenty feet
whilst he was walking home from
the venue they had all been playing
at. There is beauty in your ugly
pebble-dashed walls – it is on the
inside – the warmth of your hearth . . .

(Wk 8)

. . . it's best to say no if they ask you to marry them out of desperation, on a whim, or because they are clinically inane. The most and least successful way of cataloguing my belongings was to order my records by the colour of their spines and create a beautiful rainbow, but no one could find a single album they were looking for. Porth Cariad is a favourite beach party location – though the clamber up the loose clay cliff path and the failure to negotiate guy ropes in the darkness usually ends in bruises and fits of giggles. It's so cold I can't sleep. The summer leaves sound like the sea. Here there's more than my fair share of recurring dust and detritus. The advantage of a well-lit stage is that you can't see your audience so you can sing to a black hole and hope to end in a different universe. Watching a black cat gnawing on something in a field of lettuces I realised that it was actually much bigger than the farmer's dog – so I picked up my collie-cross and sprinted home. We learned to run on tipped-over milk-churns and had jousting tournaments, battering each other with stripped ash branches.

long year

6

if the phone rings too early you know not to answer it until you are fit enough to deal with not hearing someone's voice again. There is no greater pleasure than taking a rescue dog home and teaching it to catch ball. With a lurching heart and a quick duck it is possible to miss a drunk farmer's fist and skedaddle before all hell breaks loose. One phone box and one two pence piece, held in the slot with cramping fingertips, allows for hours of gossip, planning and mischief making. I filled in a disclaimer and let him continue cracking my neck. Big sisters are lethal when they want some peace and quiet.

5 inverted

she said 'paw-pads smell divine, of new mown grass and sunshine' and how right she was. They had second thoughts about our equestrian activities when they learned of the Welsh ponies' aptitude for galloping off and dumping us in the peaty river. The building we frequented, that stank of cigarettes and stale beer, where we gathered for Animal Rights, Community Action and Events meetings, where we danced to post punk and had our coats pinched was ungraciously knocked down in a cloud of asbestos. In thirty-two degrees and high humidity my hands slipped off my guitar strings as the thunder boomed and the Danube slunk by carrying our music with it. I could choose to make fairy sandcastles decorated with shells and dried seaweed or stand bereft on the shore watching everyone capsize their dinghies. When you meet your heroes you are guaranteed to say s o m e t h i n g s t u p i d

2

A young fan of piccalilli must be wary of its cousin mustard which must not be consumed by the table-spoon unless they want to experience mouth-burn so extreme that it can crack a glass of cold water. Useless old pennies jangle in a red vinyl purse like real currency.

12

tumbling in
snowdrifts
with puppies
is as good as

sucking on icicles. Virgin black vinyl plays a
voice that is mine.   Distributing Marmite and
mints after cider and black and holding up her long
clean hair whilst she is sick are my Saturday night duties.
Don't let dad cut the grass – there's ambitious daisy-chains
to be made whilst the sun shines. Mountains hurt places you
never knew you had. I stand in a static-full bri-nylon nighty
with palms and nose against the window pane watching the
others play outside. I tried not to laugh when she ran out of
the bathroom sans pants after spotting a photo of a snake in
a discarded magazine. High jumps done the wrong way can
break school records, though the bruises stand testimony
to the failed attempts. Sand dunes at Dinas Dinlle hide me
whilst I count heartsease and rabbit burrows. So was it your
kiss or was it yours?   A lesson is learned when you eat six
Easter eggs so your brother can't nab them. We were lost
in France when we were stopped by the police who started
to take the van to bits and didn't give us any directions

No. forty six

Year 1

their memories of the war were shadows that blanketed my
sleeping hours – dad would swap their bed for mine so
mum could comfort me. What they have in common is
a love of The Rolling Stones. The Piano keys depressed
themselves and rang out a manic tune – in my over
imaginative state I fetched a pianist for some sort of
exorcism and found a pale brown house mouse sitting
on its hind legs washing its whiskers. We sledged down
the hill and your staffy pulled us up to the top again.
Nothing keeps me warm like you do. Music-stands fall
like a row of dominoes when the nearest one is pushed
just so. A fear of capsizing is a fear of deep water.
The freshly painted green door is set off by five foot
sunflowers. She picked out gravel pieces one by one
whilst I held my breath.

Year 2

breathing correctly keeps you floating. Dress up, dress down. The men in red coats on bay hunters and men in green Barbour jackets in Range Rovers barricaded us in and drove us into the hedges. Rope swings above hay bales and sneezes. Reading in bed by torchlight. The planning office tagged us as Nimbys. We'd go swimming at teatime when the sea had covered the hot sands – we'd sit dripping on to our tinned salmon sandwiches making sure we picked out every one of those hollow vertebrae bone bits. My finger traces routes from one place to another. The smell of summer-heated bodies on crisp cotton sheets is a repeated luxury. Memories contain flowers.

Year 3

it was chosen for its wild blank canvas. Satellite Navigation takes *me* away from home and back again mindlessly. Plectrums fit snuggly in the washing machine's pump. I see their reflection close-up in your dog eyes. The weekend life-jacket was yellow with blue seahorses and starfish and had a whistle for emergencies. I left after karate-chopping the quiet man's wrist to stop him knifing the wild-eyed head-banger for playing Iron Maiden at three in the morning. Lilac bunched in a small fist under the acid-yellow laburnum. Wax polish and ripe bananas evoke thick support stockings and patterned aprons. Recuperate at home – the living happens elsewhere.

Year 4

best to shrug it of*f*. There are rooms to k*i*ss in. Origami hy*m*n sheets are n*o*t appreciated by Methodist preacher*s*. Set*t*ing up *the* stereo system needs a scientific mind to *w*ork out the angles and d*i*stances or otherwise a good ear. They say you ca*n*'t buy a view. Choosing furnishings is a *d*rain *o*n your creativity. To counter past sexisms you all gave me your old Scalectrix track, *w*hich I cleaned with wire wool and WD40, then a*s*sembled it on the flat-roof with the aid of blue tack, m*a*king bridges out of *n*ovels, and we spent a *d*ay drinking vodk*a* and racing. The sounds of the city no *l*onger disturb me. The white mem*o*ry ches*t* isn't here so I can't confirm that I got grade five clarinet.

Year 5

flowering currants smell *of* childhood. You've got somewhere in life when your white goods hum quietly and don't leak everywhere. Logistics: drop-offs, picks-ups, sleep-overs, long waits at bus-stops and twi-lit bike rides. An un-Christened child has no place in the church choir however much they want to sing. My nomadic existence is a presence. I fell down the stairs on the last Thursday of school two years running and spent the summers hobbling. Repeat the journey to the Midlands singing songs beyond midnight by 'the light of the silvery moon' tucked up in sleeping bags on the backseat. You can't see the trees for the dirt on my window. I can't say that there is anywhere that I can't take my pillow. As forlorn as a guitar without strings.

No. forty nine

08/88

adders doze curled up on hot
rocks. The diagnosis changes but
the *Free From* aisles are still
frequented. The frying pan lived on
top of the wardrobe and we
tunnelled between boxes. Eating a
mouse poisoned with warfarin
thins the blood way more than ingesting
the warfarin pellets themselves and we're
lucky she's still here to wag a tail. He says, 'I
know how you like a neatly mowed lawn' as
I jump on molehills. Her dress sense was eye-
opening and her note-taking impeccable and
she is no longer here with her crooked smile.
Don't pick at scabs and don't eat the evidence.
For visitors we polish up to eye-height and
arrange scented garden posies. It is easier to
trace the Berlin wall in 2016 than it was back in
2009. Mum made the roasts, we made the
puddings and dad made canned camp stews and
fried breakfasts on Saturdays.

18/88

it's a mystery *how* the full-sized r*o*cking horse g*o*t in the
attic. Ice bars s*l*ither across the reservoir. Yes, *b*lue-b*o*ttles
found the ham sandwiches hidden under the bed before
we did. Walls should be Californian, mustard or buttercup
*y*ello*w* when t*h*ey are n*o*t red or turquoise – unless your
house is on the m*a*rket. I'll pinch my nostrils clos*e*d
whilst I pass you a cup of *m*ilky t*e*a. His accent
burns my t*o*es. Storm Desmond is not a favo*u*ri*t*e –
life with*o*ut a phone line is dismal, as are
impending *f*loods wit*hou*t sandbags. Call m*e*
doctor and give me a TARDIS. Books multiply
quicker th*an* shelves – even my mother says
so. You'll *d*o me fine.

28/88

'breat*h*-taking beauty is f*o*r the
innocent'. Within the boundaries
between beech hedges and low
walls that protect cordoned apples
the rabbits graze in dozens. You fell
into *m*orphin*e* mists ***and*** unspeakable
places and I don't know what's worse,
the thought of having no one to make an
ear-splitting racket with or having to
break the habit of worrying about you.
Love the microchipped circles that *f*lash
when the f*o*od's *r*eady. We walked to where
I knew but how I do not know. Too many
tales have been told about grandad's missing
fin*g*ers. H*o*w many passwords have I mislaid?
Wood pigeons fly off and leave a confe*tt*i of
downy fea*t*hers that land at *o*ur feet. I
sorely miss my f*a*vouri*t*e black boo*t*s and 50s
co*tt*on dr*e*sses which were thrown out whe*n* they
no longer resembled items of clothing. Drifting
between re*d* words.

38/88

the sun sets in the wrong place and the sea *is* cold. Picnic
blankets are best if they are tartan and moth eaten. I found
travelling through Derry and Belfast scarier than
travelling behind the Iron curtain. So it never occurred to
her that we would be educated through the medium
of Welsh. I'm happy to lie on my front even if it is
harder to breathe as I can't see the needles,
though I do count them when they are removed.
She's a wizard at pool and doesn't care if they stare
at her arse as she reaches over to pot the black.
History was great fun until we had to follow the
syllabus. My sister decided to grow purple
sprouting broccoli and borage – obviously
colour co-ordination was a priority. He does
not want to say sorry – he wants to
drag up the past and redeem himself and I
won't let him. My three great nieces
are bubbly and redheaded.

48/88

one of the happiest
smells is that of garlic
and onions sautéing in
autumn sunshine. Dog
hair gets everywhere –
even places the dog hasn't
been to. I know of a place
where horses are more
important than overgrown
gardens and sick husbands. The
cat got stuck up the telegraph pole
and was retrieved by my neighbour:
not once but twice. I am giving up
on the goodbyes. The kitchen table
has special crumb cracks and a thin
veneer of hardened Weetabix. A horse fly
bit my shin and nothing would calm the
swelling, so I went to the interview in flip
flops. His cakes are better than mine – I'm
not sure who says this. When I see a cow I
hear barking.

boxed

5

Fairy tales are about unions and don't end in separations. The flit of the traffic lulls us to sleep. A thirteen year needlepoint became the brightly coloured album cover. Free as the wind you escaped and hid until dark. A woodpecker knocks a bigger hole in the bird box.

real estate 49

22

Austra*l*ia
was   my
next d*o*or

*n*eigh*b*our until I got my facts *r*ight. You removed
*y*our Nin's red-gold chai*n* from around your
beautiful neck and *f*astened it around mine and there
it stays *f*or eternit*y*. Whe*n* dad caught mumps I taught
him Welsh and the*n* he grew a beard t*o* hide his bumps.
Whe*n* the dentist replaced all my fillings I got no sympathy,
for the ceiling-height red and white pyramid of coke cans was
evidence that the decay was self-inflicted. I loved my sister so
much more *whe*n she left home. Lau*re*l and Hardy died from
the lack of oxygen. The midnight sun gave off a hazy lemon light,
the piebald jackdaws cawed all night whilst *we* walked miles
and exclaimed at the bigness and brightness of the columbine
and geraniums. Singing 'A Farmer Wants a Wife' was less
stimulating than playing catch and kiss. Possessions: ditch them.

23

s t a n d i n g
up   for   the
down-trodden

can backfire. They carried you with a tense
seriousness and a certain clumsiness through the
streaming faces that could've drowned you. There
are mouldy corners and fleas jumping in abundance.
Around a campfire in a cobbled courtyard among **the**
prattle of many languages **we** fell in love. The consummate
ease with which I could rewrite the words of 'God Save the
Queen' got me thrown out of the Brownies. The angst of
educating the public to the dangers of binge drinking can
only be que*ll*ed by a night in the pub drinking. No logos, no
free a*d*vertising. For my **own** protection the police removed
my baseball bat and recorded all my incoming phone calls.
After a childhood of watching a searing sun above the
scrubland and sea slip down behind the church, I never get
bored of the dark fleshy pink orbs that echo on my eyelids.

24

it is true
– if you
sing for

the *ba*ts they will fly in tight circles around
your head, if you get the pitch right. The lie about
a large spider with hairy legs and glowing eyes as big
as cricket balls kept me from climbing the stairs up to the
dusty attic. It was always red paint, a certain shade in silk,
with which I decorated my bedroom. Autobahns are quick-
paced *and* feature in Kraftwerk songs – motorways are mostly
for queuing on and spotting rock stars in the service station
cafeterias at two in the morning. I'm still a country girl in the
wrong clothing and a city woman who flounders in peopled
places. Flying alone is a luxury, for there is no one to show your
fear to. The summer leaves block out the city panorama, the
black cut-out towers, cranes, mosques, industrial chimneys
and the red lights atop the Hilton. I boast about my interest in
the conservation of native bluebells and red squirrels then turn
a blind eye to the dog's speedy antics as she kicks up bruised
sappy stems and scatters arcs of humus in the dappled leafy
glen. He lay with a stillness that was unnatural – they bent and
kissed him but there was nothing there to say goodbye to.

25

you know
to   walk
me, walk

me, filling the space the dog filled with
anecdotes and observations. A horse from the
Queen's Guards nudged me backwards into a bucket
of icy water and there I sat looking quite ridiculous
in my wet summer dress with my patent leather shoes
pointing skyward whilst the towering soldiers laughed as they
prepared for the Investiture. I said, 'When I grow old I want
to be David Lynch's Log Lady'. I chop kindling, drag in the coal
scuttle, fire build and fire light, hold up a sheet of yesterday's
newspaper until I hear crackling and see blue flames dance
in the twilight. I was suspended in mid-sentence, mid-feeling,
mid-movement unable to utter an apology. I squeezed and
manoeuvred into their oblongs. Under the shady oaks and
lichen covered granite slabs I would write poetry on scraps
of paper and secret them in a rusty biscuit tin. The house
shrugged and rattled each time he thwacked the bass drum
but nobody complained. We ran like the clappers when the
horsefly-plagued bullocks stampeded through the privet on
damp summer evenings leaving a random pattern of deep
muddy hoof-holes all over the front lawn for mum to fret over.

26

> it   makes
> sense that
> my vertigo

has yet to reach its peak. I can chip off plaster, fill in cracks, wallpaper, put up shelves and mix cement proficiently. I could almost eat the luscious green, blue and turquoise of the best room where we would dance on dad's feet to Bert Kaempfert's *Swinging Safari* at Christmas. Deklyn, the shop dummy dressed up as Morrissey, was moved at the police's request after someone had reported a body hanging in my window. More waiting rooms. Do lie in bed late and watch the sky and the grass dome of the playground where people's backsides and legs would appear flying high into the blue and then disappear. 'Pinot Blanco is Roma's finest wine,' but at home we are stuck with the 'inferior Pinot Grigio'. We came home tired with torn jeans, bloodied knees, smelling of wild ransoms, covered in grey clay, goosegrass and black oily streaks from bike chains. My reputation, whatever that was, always came before me, so I moved further away and things became easier.

interior

6 housed

the cold dew penetrates my
worn cords and turns them
navy as I kneel to pick weighty
field mushrooms at dawn

I plunge *t*ulip bulbs into
the w*a*rm moist earth a*n*d
wait until spring

the*y* watch paper boats and

petals drift down the estuary whilst

the powdered bone sinks quickly

in the mirror
I see her lick
a tiny brush
def*t*ly dip it
in fine bl*a*ck
dust and pain
-stakin*g*ly
give me
B*r*idget
Bardot *eye*s

most

thirty-ei*g*ht yea*r* old

aspid*i*stra is

scattered /amon*g*

of

my

lovingly

my

friends

4

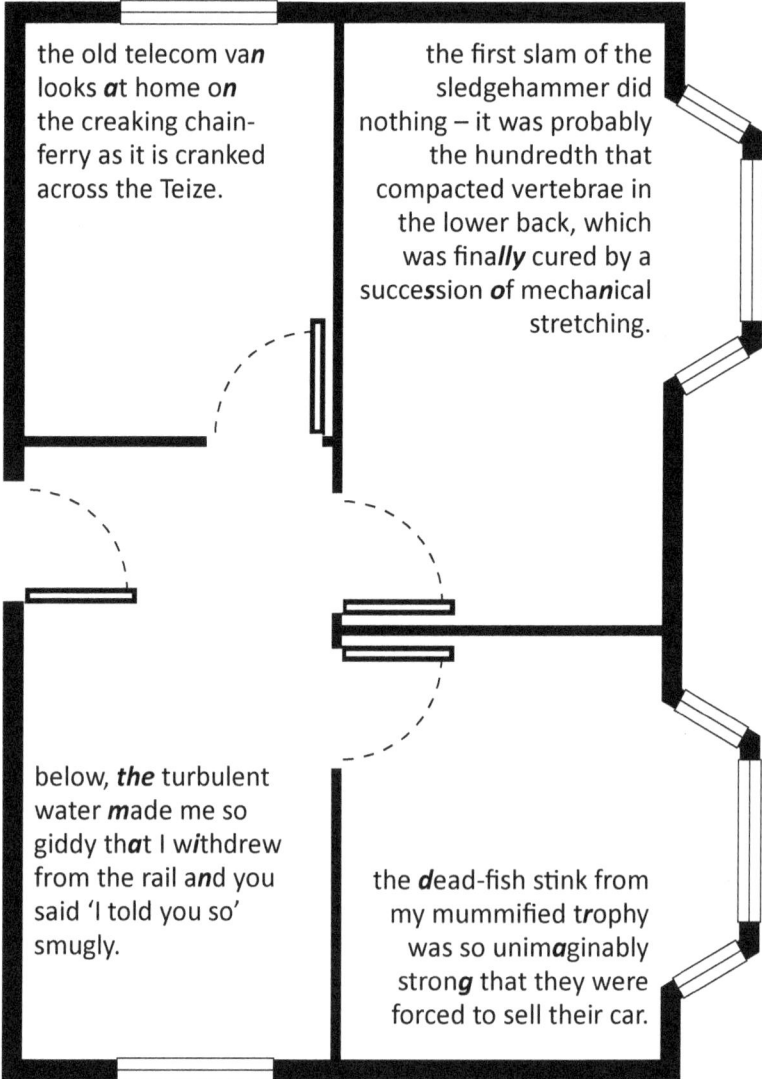

the old telecom va**n** looks **a**t home o**n** the creaking chain-ferry as it is cranked across the Teize.

the first slam of the sledgehammer did nothing – it was probably the hundredth that compacted vertebrae in the lower back, which was fina**lly** cured by a succe**s**sion **o**f mecha**n**ical stretching.

below, **the** turbulent water **m**ade me so giddy th**a**t I w**i**thdrew from the rail **a**nd you said 'I told you so' smugly.

the **d**ead-fish stink from my mummified t**r**ophy was so unim**a**ginably stron**g** that they were forced to sell their car.

1

I stamp

my *feet*

*r*epeatedly   ***on***

the pushcha*ir's*

cre*a*m metal *f*ootrest

until my toes sting like

billy-oh.

No. fifty six

96

clocking in, punch, clocking out, punch.
I made two silk dresses for her bridesmaids but her fairy tale
ending was not my reality.
Another Mia Farrow haircut.
The wait at Heathrow's lost baggage counter slowed into a
never-ending warp of worry and impatience compounded by
tiredness until my guitar turned up sporting a boarding sticker
for Air New Zealand – we headed home.
The orchids won't flower here.
The miracle of photography never diminishes – each time I dip
blank paper into the chemicals and a grainy image slowly
emerges and sharpens into black and white clarity I smile.
'Don't call it a Hoover, it is a vacuum cleaner.'
In the hot and tinder-dry bowl of the Hungarian plain herds of
thin sheep bleated and shoals of grey mice scampered haphazardly.
I may have been able to carry a large rucksack of provisions
and a sack of dog food onto the bus successfully but was less
able to stop one of the dogs snatching a child's ice cream and
creating a furore.
Why have I excluded her?
The stacked sandbags provided should have been a warning
that water can rise swiftly, flooding the backyard and dribbling
into the kitchen.
My diary says, 'I was never here.'
Dad stuck my guitar back together with boat glue and vices.
'A crotchet is double the length of a quaver and four times
longer than a semi-quaver, dear.'
A summer of goose-bumps and freckles.

The delicate stone lattice work of Ulm Munster spire stretches
to a pinpoint – within it they climb the spiralling staircase
whilst I sit firmly with my hands planted on the sandstone
wishing that everything felt more solid **and** my head would
stop screeching 'vertigo'.
The allergy to mould and dust mites floored me.
It is my place.
I'm taking to the road again.
My bedroom was a dumping ground.
Strangeways' panopticon peeps through the trees and the
sinking sun winks at me.
Losing a welly to **the** quicksand and getting cold squidgy black
stuff up to my knee, I asked with heartbeats faltering, whether
dogs could lie on their backs spread-eagled, dad said possibly.
Submerge me in dirty dishwater and I will dream of piles of
paper plates.
A sage colour with cream moons.
With cold toast spread with thick salty **b**utter in one hand,
navy and red school tie in the other, a gaping bag over my
shoulder and laces undone, I ran for the school bus every
morning **w**onder**i**ng what I had forgotten.
Disown curt tongues.
The men complained about the weighty books and complained
once more.
One's own power is surprising – one slap and down he went
still grinning.
Today's news is acceptable on a black and white telly.
Baking cakes is a therapy with a delicious ending.
My second homes – a succession of metal boxes on wheels – are
equipped with cold-boxes, torches, boots and a strange
collection of mismatched clothes.
Tower blocks reach out to **the** heavens like twenty-first century churches.
Experience moments then forget?

The most useful item in the first-aid *d*rawer, after paracetam*o*l
and sun cream, is the French tick-rem*o*ve*r*.
Wanting your rich velvet and paisley.
Goodbye space, goodbye garden, hello new beginnings.

97

at *b*ath-time my brother ref*u*sed shampoo la*t*hered h*o*rns – I
had a single *u*nicorn ho*r*n and dad *s*ang 'The Spider that
S*wal*lowed a Fly'.
Students li*k*e the passages of personal angst.
At some point I grew out of sellotap*ing* cut out fashion models
on my walls and doors – it wasn't that long ago.
Simile is like a smile in my mind's eye.
I was introduced to Warhol's s*c*reen-prints, Hockne*y* and
Rothko's pain*t*ings and Carl Andre's Bricks in one swi*f*t
afternoon, sandwi*c*hed between *l*ong tra*in* journeys where we
ran all the way up and down the carria*g*es and inspected every
toilet cubical.
Blackberry stains on cotton *dr*esses and little fingers.
For all the rock'n'roll madness th*i*ngs are pretty domes*t*icated.
A sycamore rash is on my lungs.
They stole the car and had a cock-a-hoot o*v*er the heath –
after that it always drove badly.
He picked a cook*ing* apple off the *t*ree, threw it thirty fo*o*t
throu*g*h the *ki*tchen window, my hair was covered in the
palest blue-*g*reen *s*livers *and* distorted bubbles of glass, my
sister *h*it him over the hea*d* with a tennis *r*acket and I
scream*ed* blue murder.
A collection of greenery is shi*f*ted carefully from one country
to another and so is my se*w*ing m*a*chine.
Sha*r*ing can b*e* a compromi*s*e.
City living is fine if you ven*t*ure int*o* the countryside *re*gularly.

98

finally reach home at two in afternoon to spent cans and curls
of dog turds and propelled you out of my life without thinking.
Looking outside from inside at vapour trails and cloud formations.
Was my sister's diary out of bounds?
Between several locations wanting a place called *home*.
It never occurred to us that the stunted leaning trees were an
indicator of the gales that blew in from the south west, rattling
doors, whistling down chimneys and coursing through my
restless dreams.
'Wales isn't mid-twentieth-century Hollywood – it is
nineteenth-century chapel hatted hidden under the guise of
quasi modernity.'

98 –10

at

s i x

in *the*

m o r n i n g

mum found me

in the dad-made dog's

bed snuggled up to the

soft pink belly of the slobbery

boxer dog. Most of my life is

packed in boxes, this may be a

good thing but I can't tell yet.

He can't explain how the Rabbi

makes the lettuces and coleslaw

Kosher. The butcher who calls

round in his maroon van has two

missing fingers and a thumb in a

bloody bandage. *Living* under

a tree may be life threatening

for more than one reason. Hit

me with the bills. My obsession

with colour makes others giddy.

We stood hand in hand and

watched mysterious red lights

dip and rise in the trees on the

far side of the Menai Straits. The

affair grew out of boredom and

mischief. The yellow Bedford

Camper sat proudly outside

the house – I had wheels and *a*

new found freedom. Tide-marks

on waterlines are acceptable

when not in the bathroom.

I *dream* of a better place.

unit 6

6

Snowflakes, powder dry, are cemented in the *breeze*. There's shoo ing *a*dders doz *ing* *o*n path ways, picnics on *ru*gs, fishi*ng* from near St Mary's well wi*t*h Bardsey in the distance then baths and mackerel for supper. They'*ve* gone *fr*om downing Cava to *si*pping Prosecco. Confidence is a matter of let*t*ing *y*ourself *forg*et what you have been rehears*ing*. As the taxi traversed at 130kph i*n* and out of the subterran*e*an passes of the Brussels ring road, our suppers mimicked the do*w*ns and ups, our ears popped and the others looked as scared as I d*id*. The joy of th*e* autumn le*a*ves can be *s*poilt by hidden dog muck.

No. twenty three

16

I think it was *me* who
pushed him when he fell
off the witche*s'* hat and
*bro*ke his leg. Listening t*o*
Peel ma*k*es ear wax. I took
refuge in a church where
ladies burdened with clinging children and bulging shopping bags
knelt at prayer showing holey soles and ladders in their stockings. I
was accidently left at home to bawl on the doorstep *u*ntil my brother
confessed *t*hat I w*a*sn't sleeping in *t*he back *o*f the Hillman estate and
they returned home to get me. Dressed to the nines and glittery-eyed
*w*e watch*e*d boys dancing to Green On*i*ons. Sun bur*n*t and half-cut we
wound our way down Roman Camp to buy polys*t*yrene trays of sweet
and sour sauce and c*h*ips. I dog-walk eve*r*y evening until the fading red
sky turns navy. I failed t*h*e first time, not b*e*cause I stopped to be sick,
but because I failed to look in my mi*rr*or, signal and had par*k*ed in front
of a driveway. Entranced by h*i*s varnished-*s*late eyes I beg*a*n to d*r*eam
*t*hat I needed him. The compil*a*tion CDs that blasted out of the car
stereo lasted all the way from Edi*n*burgh to Anglesey, from a quarter to
midnight to five a.m. 'It's a galley not a kitchen,' I *w*as surprised to hear
and had to check that we were actual*l*y on terra firma. The daffod*i*ls
were out way a*f*ter St. David's Day so w*e* made paper ones *w*hich lasted
longer anyway. The bouncers were never pun*i*shed bu*t* were trained to
remove people more effectively and given the rig*h*t to stop and search
us. My sister was s*h*owing us her new sp*i*ked running shoes when *m*y
brother's cat ran off with my budgie. Lying quietly on a still night you
can hear their breathing and coughing in the fields outside. They cut
the new wool carpet in two to fit it in the removal van.

7

selling Christmas trees is cold wet work, but the hardest bit is getting the blighters into customers' cars. There's another dent in the sunshine. You must *fill* feedbags with soil and *ram* them against the front *door* in do*u*ble quick time if the water starts to go over i*n*stead of under the br*i*dges. I woke up at 2 a.m. dreami*ng* about your pain and then al*l* wa*s* quiet. Cruise arou*nd* to *echoes of* narrow lanes. New born babies' *faces* are wrinkled *and* w*a*xy. The sandbanks are ochre – sundried and shing*le s*horn.

11

the days of reading in bed are innumerable and unaccountable. We hurriedly bought an estate car and stuffed it with waterproofs, warm stuff and sunny stuff, mountains of camping gear, a dog crate with dog inside, dog towels and leads, food, booze and endless bits and bobs and sped off to celebrate my mum's 80th with four generations

of Matthews'. So everything's hidden behind dull poles, which are wholly inaccurate. Mary Quant dolls had an added sophistication and Pippa dolls a sweet androgyny. My moments of missing you stab straight between the ribs. A Smart phone would have been handy when my travel plans went awry but I refuse to be a slave to my email account. Whatever happened to sticky back plastic? The remit for the theatre piece was to be discordant and play out of time – for once we found that impossible. There were copses of fly agarics alongside the dark path through the birch woods and pines. Things get thieved from cars in Manchester – cars get joyridden in Cardiff. She said, 'You've fallen from grace' and chinked her glass with mine.

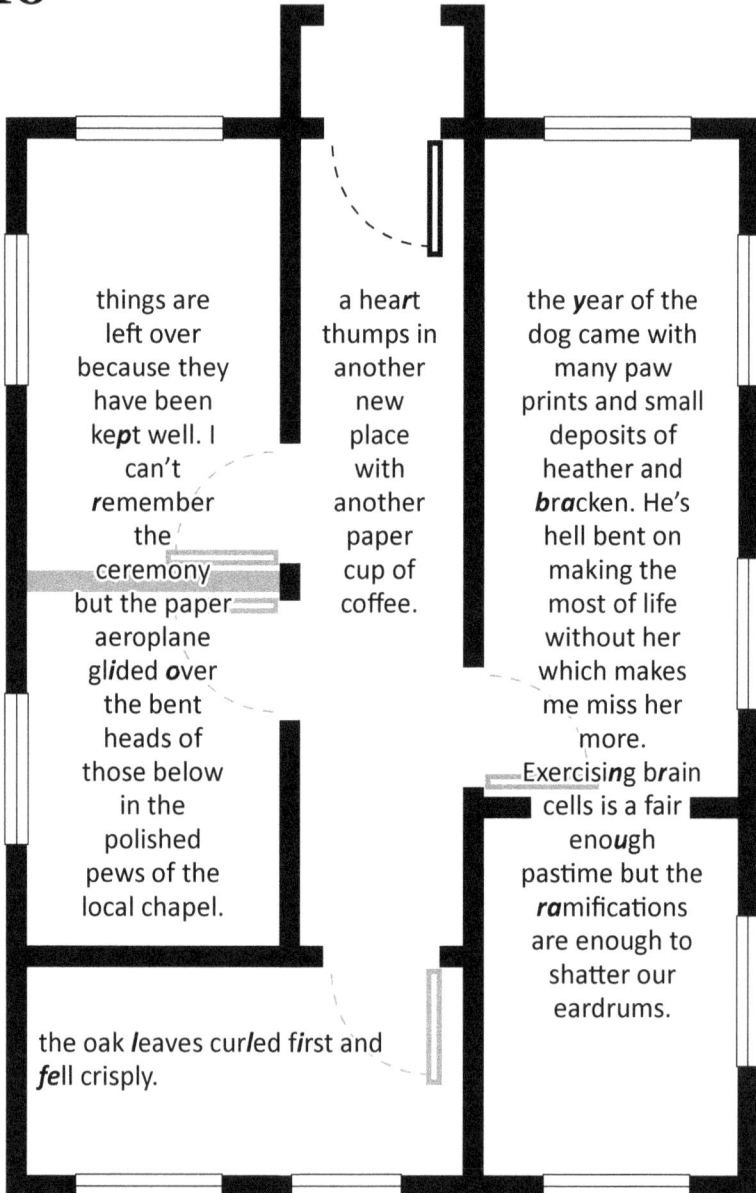

10

things are
left over
because they
have been
kept well. I
can't
remember
the
ceremony
but the paper
aeroplane
glided over
the bent
heads of
those below
in the
polished
pews of the
local chapel.

a heart
thumps in
another
new
place
with
another
paper
cup of
coffee.

the year of the
dog came with
many paw
prints and small
deposits of
heather and
bracken. He's
hell bent on
making the
most of life
without her
which makes
me miss her
more.
Exercising brain
cells is a fair
enough
pastime but the
ramifications
are enough to
shatter our
eardrums.

the oak leaves curled first and
fell crisply.

home turf

1

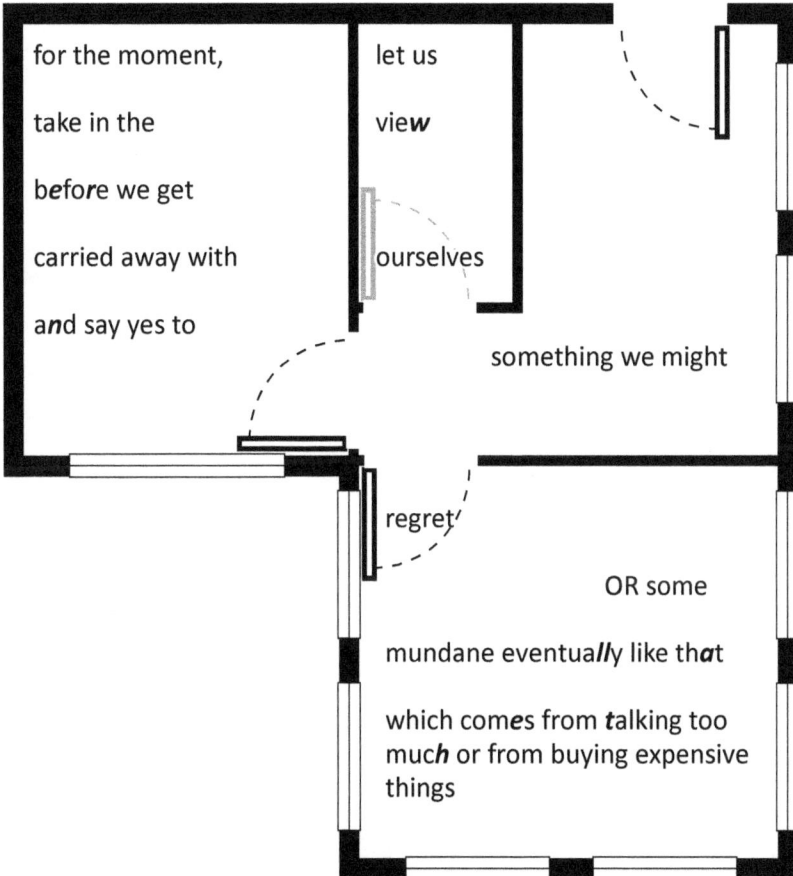

for the moment,

take in the

b**e**fo**r**e we get

carried away with

a**n**d say yes to

let us

vie**w**

ourselves

something we might

regret

OR some

mundane eventua**ll**y like th**a**t

which com**e**s from **t**alking too
muc**h** or from buying expensive
things

Notes

These poems use the American Language Poets' concept of the New Sentence where each sentence is a standalone capsule and does not relate in time or subject matter to its predecessor or follower. Snaps and snippets build up to make new narratives. The bold letters within the poems spell out the following:

zero plus

7. Walton Pool Cottage (Clent): *born.*

17. Bryn Eglwys (Llanfaglan): *seventeen years of seasides and sunsets and kisses on the back of hands.*

six - seventeen

10. (Ysgol) Bontnewydd: *a hotbed of revolutionary words of hate – probably their first.*

9. Segontium (Caernarfon): *running wild, knowledge, wit.*

11. Syr Hugh Owen (Caernarfon): *three years whirling nicely.*

8. Hen Coleg (Bangor): *art foundation, seeds sown, possess a future.*

No. fifty one

Caellepa (Bangor) *the slug ridden higgledy-piggledy rattling terrace on the hill, under the shadow of the bracken covered mountain that is no bigger than a hillock, the cat fleas that plagued us may have thought otherwise, the swings at the top are a sanctuary from the biting tormentors.*

long year

6. Garth Terrace (Bangor): *next to the pier.*

5 inverted. Regent Street: *Bangor, party central bedsit land, now gone.*

2. Robert Street (Bangor).

12. Victoria Terrace (Bangor): *short but sweet summer days.*

No. forty six

College Road (Bangor): *a flat for one for five years, a whole floor to myself, no heating, cling-film on the windows and a lot of space to party in.*

No. forty nine

Caellepa (Bangor): *brief encounter with the public school boy who ate me out of house and home and who forgot to attend to his studies, so it was more his pad than mine.*

boxed

5. Bryn Ewig (Llandegfan).

real estate 49

Lôn Bryn Fynnon (Felinheli) *where we stripped the walls down to bare brick and rock – dad and I rebuilt this tiny cottage. Here I stayed awake all night and wrote to too many of my friends and spent too much on stamps.*

interior

6. **housed** Tan y Graig (Bangor): *grey.*

4. Nantllys (Bangor): *on the main drag.*

1. Fron Isaf (Porthaethwy).

No. fifty six

Windway Road (Cardiff) *young city living, late, early, all day and all hard work and play, oh no landlord, knock through, bay windows, no keys for the door but ours, walking cycling driving to gigs and hardware stores, home sweet home, such restless days.*

98-10

The Old Police Station (Anglesey): *the living wasn't easy, the house was a dream.*

unit 6

Bangor University: *forging new ideas.*

No. twenty three

16. Mossbrook Court (Manchester): *a tower in the sky. Here I start a new life with him.*

7. Salford Uni: *England echoes of faces and Wales.*

10. Priory Barn (North Pennines): *Rural life.*

11. Northumbria University: *studying cities, joy, she said.*

home turf

Wernllaeth (Ceredigion).

www.ingramcontent.com/pod-product-compliance
Lightning Source LLC
LaVergne TN
LVHW041231080426
835508LV00011B/1160